Miss Brain's

Cool Math Games

for kids in grades 1-2

by Kelli Pearson

A Note About the Games in This Book

Many of these games have been around awhile—some for decades, others for much longer. Some have been played all over the world. One I picked up in Brazil; another is apparently a big hit with kids in El Salvador. I created a few of the games from scratch and tweaked several others to make them better as math games, but in large part I am indebted to the anonymous game makers and game players who have enjoyed them at home, on playgrounds, and in classrooms for years.

Miss Brain's Cool Math Games has taken these kid-tested games—most of which are not known as "learning games" but are just played for fun—and grouped them according to the math area they naturally teach. If a person could play fun games while also learning something they really needed to know, wouldn't that be the best of both worlds? That is what I have endeavored to do in creating this book.

My sincerest thanks to all those individuals who have created these games, all who have played them, and all who have passed them on to others. Great games bring us together, make us happy, and (if we're lucky) even teach us something!

ISBN: 978-0-9855725-0-1

Growing Smart Kids
1050 Kiely Blvd.
PO Box 3263
Santa Clara, CA 95055

http://www.coolmathgamesforkids1-2.com

Table of Contents

Introduction

Number Sense

Whose is Greater?	*Twins*
Dozens Dice	*Guess Odd, Guess Even*
Odd and Even Beans	*Giganto-score*
The Odd-Even Game	*Roundit*

Counting

Pig	*Tally Marks*
Make 10	*Take It to Ten*

Addition

Subtraction

Place Value

Money

Fractions

Multiplication

Appendix

Introduction

- ✦ Parents: Helping Kids With Math

- ✦ Teachers: Using Games in the Classroom

- ✦ How Can Games Help Kids Learn?

- ✦ Your Math Learning Tool Kit

- ✦ Math Overview

- ✦ Some Thoughts About Materials

Parents: Helping Kids With Math

A lot of parents get a little freaked out at the thought of explaining fractions to a 7-year-old.

It's understandable. After all, a good number of us adults have a few math anxiety issues. Most parents aren't sure even where to start when helping kids with math. And when your kid whines, "That's not how my *teacher* said to do it!"—well, that's just the icing on the cake.

Here's the good news: helping your child get better at math doesn't have to be so hard. With this book, you can help your child understand first and second grade math, and all you have to do is play games together.

Don't be fooled: just because games are fun doesn't mean they are frivolous. We tend to think that when kids are playing, they are not learning, and vice-versa. But kids can and do learn through play, and believe it or not, having fun can even help kids learn *better*.

The games in this book help kids practice math without really seeming to. Each game gives kids practice with a particular math skill, or a few related skills, so they can give all their attention to mastering that one thing. The more they play, the more they will improve.

It's time to say good-bye to fighting with math. Watch your kids' confidence soar as they win games using their new math skills. Laugh and play together as a family. And go ahead and smile to yourself when you hear your first or second grader utter those remarkable words: "I *love* math!"

Teachers: Using Games in the Classroom

Let's face it: game-playing hasn't traditionally been a big part of the math classroom. But more and more teachers are realizing the power of play—not just as a way of blowing off steam, but also as a tool for helping kids learn.

Games also happen to be a great bridge between home and the classroom. Teachers often encourage parents to work with their children at home, but it can be hard to know where to begin or exactly what to do. Teaching parents a simple math practice game makes it easy for them to help their kids improve.

I wrote this book as a resource for both parents and teachers, but I did have to make some choices around language: do I refer to "your class" or "your child"? In the end, I settled on language which is most welcoming for parents, since parents have so few resources for teaching their kids, but the games are great for small group work and learning centers in school as well.

You won't need a lot of fancy materials. Almost all of the games can be played by kids of mixed abilities, so that kids who are better in math won't have a winning advantage over kids who are a bit slower. And best of all (in the eyes of the kids, at least) Miss Brain's Cool Math Games are seriously fun to play!

Get ready to see your kids' eyes light up as you make game time a part of class time. I promise you, once you see your struggling kids pestering you for more math practice, you'll be hooked.

How Can Games Help Kids Learn?

First off, let's clarify: a game is not a teacher. If a child hasn't heard of odd and even numbers, then playing a game with odd and even numbers is not going to be fun, it'll just be frustrating. Kids need to be at least somewhat familiar with a concept before it makes sense to play a game with it.

However--there are many steps to learning, and once kids have been introduced to a new math concept, their work is just beginning. Once they have begun to understand how something works, they need to test it out, see how it works in their world, and (most of all) practice it.

That's where games come in.

I am convinced there is no better tool than a good math game to help kids practice what they are learning. Games use kids' whole bodies, which gets new parts of their brain involved. Games relax and energize them so they want to play (and in this case practice) over and over.

Studies have shown that we are much more likely to remember something when our emotions are involved. When something is dull, even though we might understand it, it is all too likely to slip out of our heads. But if we feel excited, suspenseful, happy--that learning is more likely to stick.

Math games make kids more open to learning, motivate them to keep practicing new skills, and help them remember what they learn.

Your Math Learning Tool Kit

Miss Brain's Cool Math Games brings you the tools you need to help your kids make sense of math, practice it, and have fun with it.

Each game is carefully chosen to reinforce just one math skill. When kids are learning a new math concept, they need lots of opportunities to focus on just that skill and perfect it. The games are grouped according to math area, with the more basic math concepts located at the front of the book.

Because kids will be practicing new skills while playing the games, they may need your support and coaching as they work toward mastering tricky concepts. *Miss Brain's Cool Math Games* starts off each new chapter with an overview that gives practical tips on how to help your child with that specific math area.

You will also learn which specific skills kids need in order to master each math area. This is not as obvious as you might think. One math area might require 4 or 5 different skills that kids need to develop one at a time. As you become aware of the math your kids are learning, you'll be more equipped to help them over each new hurdle.

Some of the vocabulary used in this book may not be familiar to you, since they are "teacher terms" that are not often used in everyday life. Take a few minutes to look through the glossary in the back of the book. It makes these terms easy to understand, and will also help you explain new words and ideas (like "odd and even numbers") to your kids.

Math Overview

Each chapter starts with a summary and explanation of the skills kids need to understand that math concept. The games, tips and information in this book will help kids master the following math areas and skills:

Number Sense: naming numbers, comparing numbers, odd and even numbers, sequencing numbers, rounding numbers

Counting: counting to 1,000, counting on, counting back, skip counting

Addition: counting on, adding doubles, making 10, the flip-it-around rule

Subtraction: fact families, counting back, counting on, finding doubles, finding tens

Place Value: reading larger numbers, comparing numbers, naming place value, regrouping

Money: identifying coin values, skip counting, counting on, putting coins in order, mixing counting skills, adding and subtracting, regrouping

Fractions: concept of equal parts, recognizing fractions, reading fractions, comparing fractions, ordering fractions

Multiplication: concept of equal parts, skip counting, language of multiplication, writing multiplication problems, multiplication facts

Some Thoughts About Materials

I've kept materials simple with *Miss Brain's Cool Math Games*. If you have a deck of playing cards, a couple of dice, and some other common household items, you are ready for most of the games in this book:

- ✦ 2 dot dice
- ✦ playing cards
- ✦ paper and pencil
- ✦ paper bags
- ✦ rubber bands

- ✦ bag of rice
- ✦ measuring scoop
- ✦ empty egg cartons
- ✦ graph paper
- ✦ counters (such as dried beans)

A few games call for special materials that help kids learn a particular concept. Some examples are:

✦ fraction strips

| 1/2 | 1/2 |

✦ place value counters

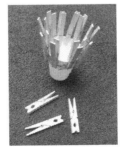

✦ coins or play money

✦ numeral dice

Other games call for printed resources, such as a hundreds chart or number line. You will find these in the Appendix at the back of the book, or you can download them from **www.coolmathgamesforkids1-2.com**. For more information about materials, visit Printables & Resources on page 69.

Math Games

- ✦ Number Sense

- ✦ Counting

- ✦ Addition

- ✦ Subtraction

- ✦ Place Value

- ✦ Money

- ✦ Fractions

- ✦ Multiplication

Number Sense: an overview

Can you picture 10 pencils in your mind? How about 50 pencils? About how much water will fill one cup? Which is more: 43 marbles or 34 marbles?

We have a sort of intuition about numbers that we develop over time. This is called number sense. The more we work with objects--hold them, count them, manipulate them--the better idea we have of quantities. When we have measured a teaspoon of vanilla in 5 or 6 batches of cookies, we get a good idea of about how much a teaspoon is.

Number sense also has to do with an understanding of the written numbers themselves. Young children have to learn that the number "4" refers to a certain quantity of objects. Later, they learn the difference between numbers like 18 and 81, and get a sense of these quantities in their heads.

The best way to develop good number sense is to give kids lots of hands-on opportunities to play with quantities and numbers. Number sense is woven into the other math areas, and can't be learned strictly on its own.

However, there are certain skills that are considered to be an important part of number sense, which can be learned and practiced individually. The most common of these are **naming numbers, comparing numbers, odd and even numbers, sequencing numbers** and **rounding numbers.**

Number Sense Skills Kids Need

Naming Numbers. Kids will learn the pattern of counting numbers (28, 29, 30 is like 88, 89, 90). They learn how numbers relate to each other (50 is ten more than 40). They also learn the names of numbers, and begin to have a sense of how many objects each number refers to.

Comparing Numbers. Which number is greater: 181 or 179? Also known as "greater than, less than", kids need to understand how numbers compare to each other, know what the words "greater than", "less than" and "equal" mean, and to understand and use the symbols <, > and =.

Odd and Even Numbers. Even numbers of objects can all be paired up; each number has a "friend". Odd numbers, when put in pairs, have one left without a friend. Until kids have memorized patterns for which numbers are odd and which are even, they will need to physically count them to see if they can be paired up.

Sequencing Numbers. If given the number 23, your child should be able to tell the next numbers that come in the sequence: 24, 25. Kids should also be able to count backwards from a number: 90, 89, 88. Second graders should be able to manipulate numbers up to 1,000 in this way.

Rounding Numbers. First and second graders will learn to round 2-digit numbers to the nearest tens place using a number line or another visual. They will learn to tell which number in the tens place is closest to their number, and round to that number.

Number Sense Games

Whose Is Greater?

Players: 2   **Skill:** compare numbers using "greater than" and "less than"

Materials: deck of cards

1. Take out the face cards (jack, queen, king) from a deck of cards, but leave aces in. Tell kids that aces are 1. Divide the deck in half between two players. Players turn their pile of cards face down in front of them.

2. Each player turns over one card at the same time. Both players compare the numbers to see which is greater.

3. The one with the greater number says a greater-than sentence about the two cards, then takes both cards. For example, if Jim turns over an 8 and Zoe has a 3, Jim says, "Eight is greater than three," and takes both cards.

4. The person with the most cards after players have gone through the entire deck wins. (Or, just stop when you get tired.)

5. CHALLENGE 1: Instead of simply saying that "8 is greater than 3", challenge players to also write 8 > 3. If written incorrectly, the other player wins that round.

6. CHALLENGE 2: During play, each child turns over two cards and arranges them to make a 2-digit number. Players compare their numbers and the one with the greater number takes all four cards.

Twins

Players: 2-3   **Skill:** naming and matching numbers

Materials: paper, pencil

1. This super-simple game is an intriguing combination of a maze and a "seek and find" challenge.

2. Get a piece of paper. Write a number anywhere on the paper. Then write the same number again in another part of the paper, some distance from its "twin".

3. Write new pairs of numbers all over the paper, until the paper is filled. I recommend using a half-sheet to start; it's easier to fill the whole thing up. Use as many numbers as you can fit.

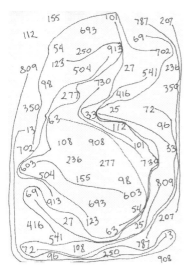

4. The first person picks a number and reads it out loud, then finds its twin and draws a line between them. Lines can be straight or curved.

5. The second person picks another number and does the same, but the new line *must not cross through any other lines*.

6. The last person who is able to connect two twin numbers without crossing a line wins.

7. CHALLENGE: Try crowding even more number pairs onto your paper, making your numbers longer, or writing similar numbers like 72, 27, 702, and 207. You can also play so that, at the end of every turn, that player tells the next person which number to find and connect.

Dozens Dice

Players: 2   **Skill:** counting, sequencing numbers, adding

Materials: dice, paper and pencil for each person

1. This addictive game is a fun mix of adding and sequencing numbers. The purpose of the game is for one person to be the first to roll the numbers 1-12 in order.

2. Before beginning, each person writes the numbers 1-12 on their paper.

3. The first player rolls both dice. If one of the dice shows a '1', the player gets to cross the number off her paper and roll again. This time she is trying for either a '2' on one of the dice, or two 'ones' (add up to 2).

4. When the player can't go any more, play passes to the next person, who tries for a '1'. Play continues in this way, with each player trying to roll the next number on their own paper.

5. Players can get their numbers either from one die, or by adding both together. So if you were trying for a 5, you could get a 5 on one die, a combination of 3 and 2, or a 4 and 1.

6. Players cannot cross off numbers out of order. The first person to get the numbers in sequence up to 12 wins.

7. CHALLENGE: When playing with higher level kids, challenge them to add the numbers together without counting the dots or their fingers. Say "5 + 6" (or whatever number is on the dice), and encourage them to use counting on, addition facts, or other addition strategies to solve.

Guess Odd, Guess Even

Players: 2+   **Skill:** identifying odd and even numbers

Materials: two dice, paper, pencil, counters (optional)

1. **NOTE:** To play this game, players need to be able to determine whether a number up to 12 is odd or even. Many kids will benefit from using counters, such as dried beans, or their fingers to see if the number can be paired. In time, they will begin to remember which are odd or even.

2. Before rolling the dice, guess out loud whether your roll will be an odd or even number.

3. Roll the dice. Figure out if the number is odd or even.

4. If a child needs to use counters to figure out if the number is odd or even, explain that even numbers all have "a friend", while odd numbers have "somebody left out". Count out enough beans for that number and put them into pairs to see if they are even or odd.

5. Did you guess correctly? If so, you get the amount of points shown on the dice. Write your score down on your paper.

6. If you guessed incorrectly, you don't get points for that roll.

7. Take turns rolling the dice. Keep track of your points each round. At the end of 10 rounds, add your points together and see who wins.

8. **COOPERATIVE VERSION:** Instead of playing in competition, play together to see how many points you can get. Write the scores of both players, and at the end of the game add up the total to see how high you got.

Odd and Even Beans

Players: 2   **Skill:** identifying odd and even numbers

Materials: 24 dried beans, two paper bags

1. Give each player a paper bag, and put 12 beans in each bag.

2. Let's say our two players are named Toby and Fatima. Fatima secretly takes some beans from her bag and hides them in her hand. She shows Toby her closed hand.

3. Toby does *not* guess how many beans she is holding; instead, he guesses if the number of beans in her hand are odd or even.

4. Fatima shows the beans in her hand. If Toby was correct, he gets to put those beans in his own bag. So if Fatima was holding 5 beans, and Toby guessed "odd", he gets to put those five beans in his own bag.

5. BUT--if Toby was wrong (if he had guessed "even"), then he would have had to give Fatima 5 beans from *his* bag, which she would then put in her own bag.

6. Players take turns guessing odd or even, and the beans will usually flow from one bag to the other quite randomly. When one person runs out of beans, the game is over.

7. CHALLENGE: Encourage older kids to use higher level skills to determine whether the number of beans is odd or even: counting up by 2's, saying an odd-even rhyme, or other methods that do not involve physically pairing up the beans.

Giganto-score

Players: 2   **Skill:** comparing numbers
Materials: number cards (page 76), pencil and paper

1. **PREP:** Print a set of number cards.

2. Turn cards face down. To play, each player takes a card. Together, they compare the numbers. Make a sentence: "38 is greater than 19".

3. The one with the greater number writes down that number as his or her score for that round. The one with the lesser number doesn't score.

4. Play for 10 rounds and add up the scores. Since you are working with higher numbers, scores will be, well, giganto! You may either need to help adding scores or let kids use calculators to find their total.

The Odd-Even Game

Players: 2   **Skill:** identifying odd and even numbers
Materials: nothing but your hands

1. Play this game when you need to decide who goes first, or who is "it".

2. There are 2 players. Decide which person is "odd" and who is "even". Each player makes one fist and together they count, 1, 2, 3.

3. On "three", each player shows some fingers on one hand. Count up the total number of fingers on both players' hands. If it is an odd number, the "odd" player wins. If even, the "even" player wins.

Roundit

Players: 2+   **Skill:** rounding numbers

Materials: number cards (page 76), number line (page 73), paper, pencil

1. Print the set of number cards, and the number line 1-100. Cut out the number line halves and tape them together.

2. Review how to count by tens. Find the numbers 10, 20, 30, and so on up to 100 on the number line.

3. Players will take turns drawing a number card and finding that number on the number line. Then they will look to see which of the "tens" numbers is closest, and write that number down as their score.

4. If the number falls exactly in the middle, such as 15, tell kids to *round up* to the next number in the tens place.

5. As you play, use phrases like **round up, round down,** or **tens place.** While this vocabulary may be new to first graders, they can easily catch on to the concept, so use this as an opportunity to start introducing the new math words.

6. Play 5+ rounds, then add up the column of numbers to find your total.

7. CHALLENGE: Once kids start feeling comfortable finding the number and rounding it on the number line, challenge them to guess what the nearest tens place will be without looking. Then, check their guess by looking it up on the number line. If they figure it out without looking, they can add another 2 points onto their score.

Counting: an overview

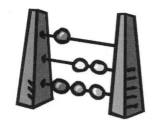

When kids are learning to count, what is really going on? At first kids use rote memory, reciting a 1-2-3-4-5 sequence they've heard. Their counting and pointing don't always match up; they are working on connecting each new object with a new number, or **one to one correspondence**.

As children learn to count higher, it becomes too hard to memorize them all and they must learn the **pattern of counting**. They discover that the cycle of 0-9 repeats over and over. At this stage, as they learn numbers up to 100 and beyond, they must also develop an idea about how many objects these larger numbers represent.

Once kids become comfortable with counting up by ones, they learn ways of counting more quickly and efficiently. Skipping over numbers in a pattern is called **skip counting**. They will also learn to **count backwards.**

Other types of counting are used as strategies in addition and subtraction, such as **counting on** and **counting back**. ('Counting back' is the skill of counting backwards from a given number.)

It is important for kids to become proficient in the various counting skills, since they will form the foundation for addition, subtraction, multiplication and division. If counting skills are strong, kids will have a much better chance of mastering the harder skills down the road.

Counting Skills Kids Need

Counting. First graders should be able to count by ones to 100, and second graders should be able to count to 1,000.

Counting On. Kids should be able to start on numbers other than 1 and count up from there. Counting on is an important skill for adding. To solve 3+24, children need to be taught to start with the larger number (24) and count on: 25, 26, 27, holding up another finger for each new number.

Counting Backwards. First and second graders should be able to count backwards from a number they are given. This is an important skill for subtraction. To solve 25-3, for example, kids start with 25, hold up 3 fingers, and count back 24, 23, 22.

Skip Counting. Skip counting is a faster way of counting that skips over certain numbers. Skip counting by 5s would be "5, 10, 15, 20" etc. First graders generally learn to skip count by 2s, 5s, and 10s, and in second grade progress to skip counting by the other numbers. Since it is the basis for multiplication, kids should become comfortable skip counting by all numbers from 2-11 by third grade (see Skip Counting reference, page 71).

Counting Games

Pig

Players: 2+   **Skill:** counting on, adding 2-digit numbers (some versions)
Materials: one or two dice, paper, pencil

1. **EASY VERSION:** Play with one die. On your turn, you can roll the die as many times as you want. Each time you roll, count on to add the additional points on to your score. There is only one catch: **if you roll the number 1, you get 0 points for that round!**

2. Play one round and write down your end score. The person with the highest score wins the round. Start from zero for the following round.

3. This is a good version to play if your child has trouble losing (since there are more chances to win), or if adding 2-digit numbers is difficult.

4. The goal is to get as many points as possible.

5. **INTERMEDIATE VERSION:** Play as above using one die, but instead of comparing scores for a "winner" after each round, play for 5 or more rounds. Adding up 2-digit numbers adds more difficulty.

6. **YIKES! VERSION:** Play with two dice. Add the numbers on the dice to get your score, and keep rolling & adding numbers as long as you dare. If you get a 1, you get 0 points for that round. But--if you roll two 1's, you lose ALL your points so far! Play 5 rounds and add up your score.

Tally Marks

Players: 1-4   **Skill:** counting by 5s, counting on
Materials: paper, pencil, 2 dice

1	I	6	⊬⊦ I
2	II	7	⊬⊦ II
3	III	8	⊬⊦ III
4	IIII	9	⊬⊦ IIII
5	⊬⊦	10	⊬⊦ ⊬⊦

1. This is a simple dice game. To get points, roll 2 dice on each turn and add your points to your total.

2. The unusual part of this game is that each person will write their score as tally marks instead of numbers. To do this, make one line for each point. The fifth point gets crossed through the previous four to make a bundle of 5 (see picture).

3. At the end of each turn, players add their new points to their score and say how many points they have so far. To count points, kids will first skip count the bundles by five, then add on the ones.

4. To count to 12, for example, show kids how to count the fives first: "5, 10" and then the ones: "11, 12".

5. The goal is to be the first to reach 50.

6. NOTE: Of course, there is really no need to count up the score at every turn. But since kids are learning to skip count by fives and add on single numbers, it's a good idea to give kids as much practice as possible. Plus, kids like knowing what their score is.

7. TAKE IT FARTHER: Mixing up skip counting with adding on ones is an important skill for counting money. Follow up this game by giving kids a mix of nickels and pennies to count. More advanced kids can add dimes, nickels, and pennies.

Make 10

Players: 1-4   **Skill:** counting, adding to make 10

Materials: playing cards

1. Tell kids that Aces = 1 and face cards (jack, queen, king) = 10. Shuffle the cards. Lay out 10 cards in a row, face up.

2. Look for cards that equal 10. Remove any card or combination of two cards that equals ten. Ex: 3+7, A+9, jack, 4+6, etc. (If you have no tens to remove, add cards until you can.)

3. Keep any cards that were removed, then fill in the holes with new cards.

4. Take turns playing until all the cards are gone.

Take It to Ten

Players: 2+   **Skill:** counting, adding to make 10

Materials: playing cards with face cards and 10s removed

1. Deal 7 cards to each player and put the rest face-down in the middle. The first player lays down a card. Let's say she plays a 6. (She then draws a card from the pile so she still has 7 cards in her hand.)

2. If the next player can bring the total to 10—in this case, with a 4—he plays it and takes both cards. If he can't make 10, he lays down a different card and draws one from the pile.

3. When cards run out, the person who has collected the most cards wins.

Addition: an overview

When learning to add, young children count objects, push them together, and count the total. They may count on their fingers, beginning with the number one and counting up until they reach the total.

First and second graders are beginning to work with larger numbers, and need to go beyond simple counting strategies in order to solve them. They need to add written problems that involve 2- and 3-digit numbers, and memorize their addition facts.

In addition to **memorizing addition facts**, they need to learn adding strategies such as **counting on**, **adding doubles**, **making ten**, and what we'll call the **flip-it-around rule.** These strategies will give kids new ways of solving problems in their heads, and will help them add more quickly.

Many kids will find it helpful to have dried beans or other objects available to count when playing these games. First and second graders are working on memorizing math facts, so encourage them to try to add simple sums in their heads or to think of the facts they have been learning.

Children also need to learn addition vocabulary. When talking with kids during your games, use words like "add", plus", and "equals". Ask about their "sum" (the answer to an addition problem). If kids hear these words used often in context, they will use them on their own quite naturally.

Addition Skills Kids Need

Counting On. When given a number other than 1, kids should be able to continue counting from that number. The counting on strategy is used when at least one of the numbers in the problem is smaller than 10, since the added-on numbers are counted on fingers.

Always start with the larger number and count on from there. For example, if solving 3+14, start with 14 (larger number) and count three more by showing three fingers: 15, 16, 17.

Adding Doubles. 2+2, 3+3, and 4+4 are examples of doubles. Learning all the doubles (from 1+1 to 10+10) makes it easier for many children to memorize those facts. Practice addition doubles together as you cook, drive, or whenever you have a spare minute.

Make Ten. Kids need to develop a solid knowledge of which numbers add up to ten: 1+9, 2+8, 3+7, 4+6, and 5+5, as well as their reverse. This skill is helpful in learning math facts, and will be very useful when kids are adding larger numbers such as 38+2.

The Flip-It-Around Rule. 2+4 is the same as 4+2, but young kids don't get this at first, even thought it seems obvious to you. They need lots of opportunities to move objects around and find out for themselves that the totals really are the same. Remind kids of this rule if they know that 9+1=10 but are struggling with 1+9, for example. Eventually it will "click".

Addition Games

Bull's-Eye

Players: 2+   **Skill:** adding, naming numbers, regrouping
Materials: paper, pencil

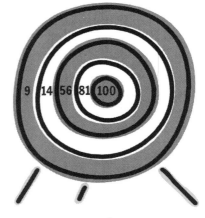

1. Start by drawing a large bulls-eye, big enough to fill a piece of paper. Inside each ring, write a different number, largest numbers in the center. These numbers are the points a player can get.

2. Give a pencil to one of the players and put the bulls-eye paper on the table. The player closes her eyes and lets the pencil fall somewhere onto the paper.

3. The number your pencil lands on is your amount of points for that round. Write down your score on another piece of paper.

4. Have each person play three times. Players add their three numbers together to get their score.

5. NOTE: Players should be able to do addition regrouping in order to play this game. If adding a column of numbers is too challenging, have them add two of the numbers, then add the third number to the total.

6. CHALLENGE: You can easily adjust the level of this game based on the numbers you choose to write inside the bulls-eye. More advanced kids can also play more rounds and add up longer columns of scores.

Addition War

Players: 2   **Skill:** counting, adding numbers 1-10
Materials: deck of cards

1. Explain that aces = 1 and face cards are equal to 10. Shuffle and divide the deck in half. Give each half to one person, in a face-down pile.

2. EASY, LOW-STRESS VERSION: This variation is best for kids and adults, or kids of different skill levels, since it doesn't offer an unfair advantage to more advanced players.

3. Each player turns over, at the same time, the top 2 cards of their face-down pile. The cards will be side by side on the table, facing up.

4. Each player adds the 2 cards together to get the sum. Each one says the math problem with the answer: "5+4 is 9". The one with the higher total takes all four cards--his own and his opponent's--and keeps them in his "points" pile.

5. The goal is to collect the most cards. When both players' decks are used up, count how many "point" cards you have. This is your score.

6. SPEEDY VERSION: This is actually the version that most kids prefer, but players must be at approximately the same level for it to be fair.

7. Play as above, but each player turns over one card. At the same time, players add both cards together; the first to say the correct answer out loud takes both cards and adds them to his "points" pile.

8. If both say the correct answer at the same time, each turns over one more card. The one who answers correctly keeps all four of the cards.

Shut the Box

Players: 2+   **Skill:** counting, adding numbers 1-12
Materials: paper, pencil and 2 dice

1. This quick game is a paper-and-pencil version of the traditional wooden game called 'Shut the Box'.

2. Each player writes the numbers 1-12 on a piece of paper. The goal is to be the first to cross these numbers off your paper.

3. Player 1 rolls both dice. Let's say he rolls a 2 and a 5. He can cross off his 2 and his 5, or he can cross off his 7. If these numbers are already crossed off, he skips his turn.

4. The first to cross off all the numbers on the paper wins.

Run to 100

Players: 2-4   **Skill:** counting to 100, noticing 10s
Materials: hundreds chart (page 70), 2 dice, a counter for each player

1. Print or copy a hundreds chart from the Appendix or website to use as your game board. Have each person choose a different kind of counter.

2. The first person rolls the dice and moves that many spaces on the board. Each player does the same, moving counters along like on a regular game board.

3. If a player lands on a multiple of 10, she gets to move ahead two more. The first to reach 100 wins.

Subtraction: an overview

Many kids struggle with subtraction and the concept of "difference". What is the difference between 9 and 7? What is 54 minus 3? Subtraction involves harder concepts than addition, and requires flexibility with counting both forwards and backwards.

Addition and subtraction are closely related. Being good at addition does not guarantee that a child will be good at subtraction, but being weak in addition *does* generally mean that a child will also be weak in subtraction.

This is because addition is a building block that leads to subtraction concepts, and if that foundation is shaky, everything that comes after it will be unsteady as well. If your child is struggling with subtraction, make sure she has a good understanding of counting and addition before moving on to subtraction skills.

Kids will absolutely need to understand the connection between addition and subtraction. They need a lot of practice putting a group of things together to add (5+3=8), and taking those same things apart to subtract (8-5=3). These relationships are called **fact families.**

As kids work with objects to show addition and related subtraction problems, they will begin to see how the addition strategies they learned can also help them with subtraction. **Counting on**, surprisingly enough, can be used with subtraction, too. **Doubles** and **finding tens** also come in handy with subtraction.

Subtraction Skills Kids Need

Fact Families. Every addition problem can be said to have 4 members of its fact "family". For example, 3+2=5 is related to 2+3=5, 5-3=2, and 5-2=3. Understanding how families are related makes it much easier to learn math facts; a strong knowledge of addition facts makes it easier to figure out subtraction facts without needing to count.

Counting Back. When given a number, children should be able to count backwards from it. *Counting back works when the smaller number is less than 10.* For example, in the problem 32-4, we can start with 32 and count backwards because the smaller number is less than ten.

Counting On. *Counting on is a better strategy when both of the numbers are relatively close together*, such as 54-51. To solve, start with the smaller number and count up to the second number. In this example, start with 51 and count up 52, 53, 54 while showing 1, 2, 3 fingers. The answer = 3.

Doubles. The doubles your child learned when memorizing addition facts will come in handy when subtracting numbers like 14-7 or 18-9. A simple observation that "this is a double" will usually make solving it easier.

Finding Tens. Just as making tens was important in adding, subtraction problems are also easier when kids recognize tens combinations. Even kids who know 5+5=10 will try to count backwards to find the answer to 10-5. They need to be reminded to use their math facts skills for subtraction as well as addition.

Subtraction Games

Subtraction War

Players: 2   **Skill:** subtraction, various subtraction strategies
Materials: deck of cards

1. Explain that aces = 1, and face cards = 10. Shuffle and divide the deck in half. Give each half to one person, in a face-down pile.

2. **EASY, LOW-STRESS VERSION:** Both players turn over their top 2 cards so they are side by side, face-up on the table. Put the higher card in front of the lower card.

3. Each player subtracts the lower card to get the difference. Each player says their subtraction sentence: "9-4=5". The one with the *lowest* number as the difference gets to keep all four cards.

4. The goal is to collect the most cards. When both players' decks are used up, count how many "point" cards you have. This is your score.

5. **SPEEDY VERSION:** Players must be at approximately the same level of ability for this game to be fair. To play, each player turns over one card. Players subtract the smaller number from the larger one, and try to be first to say the correct answer.

6. Have the other player "check" to make sure the answer is correct. If it is, the player takes both cards. If it is not correct, the other player gets to take both cards.

Start With Ten

Players: 2+   **Skill:** subtraction, adding a column of 5 numbers, regrouping
Materials: one die, paper, pencil, counters (optional)

1. The purpose of this game is to get the highest score after 5 rounds.

2. To play, roll the die. Subtract that number from ten to get your score for that roll. Ex: You roll a 'four'. 10-4=6 so your score for that roll is 6. On your next turn, you roll a 'one', and 10-1=9 so your score will be 9 points for that round.

3. Continue rolling and subtracting from 10 until each player has gone 5 times. Have each player add their column of 5 numbers to get their score. (You may have to help younger children with this part, or let them use a calculator.)

4. The player with the highest score wins.

5. NOTE: Observant kids will notice an interesting thing while playing this game: rolling a higher number (which is usually a good thing) in this game leads to a lower score!

6. CHALLENGE 1: After kids get the hang of subtracting from 10, play this game by subtracting from 20, 50, or 100. Their scores will also be much bigger, so they may need help adding their totals.

7. CHALLENGE 2: When subtracting from 20 or higher, you can also roll 2 dice and subtract larger numbers. This will involve subtracting numbers up to 12, which requires regrouping, so it's quite a bit more challenging.

Race to Zero

Players: 2-4   **Skill:** subtraction from large numbers, place value, regrouping
Materials: 1 die, paper, pencil, hundreds chart (optional)

1. Choose a number to start from, such as 50. Each person writes the number 50 at the top of their papers.

2. Take turns rolling one die. Each time you roll, subtract that amount from the number on your paper and write your new total. (If necessary, use the hundreds chart on page 70 and count back to get your answer.)

3. Continue until you reach zero. This can be tricky: in order to win, you must get to zero exactly. The first to get to zero wins.

What's the Difference?

Players: 2   **Skill:** subtraction from larger numbers, regrouping
Materials: number cards (page 76), one or two dice, paper, pencil

1. Print and cut out the number cards.

2. On your turn, draw a card and roll one die. Subtract the number on the die from the one on the card. Your answer is your score for that round.

3. Play five rounds and add up your score. Highest score wins.

4. CHALLENGE: Roll 2 dice and subtract that number from the one on the number card. You can also make a set of cards with higher numbers.

Place Value: an overview

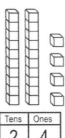

Tens	Ones
2	4

The best way to explain place value is with an example. When you look at the number 352, you know it refers to 3 hundreds, 5 tens, and 2 ones. However, young children may not understand which is bigger: 352 or 532. They are just starting to understand the concept of place value.

When kids are beginning to count, they learn that 3 is 3. Later on they learn that the numbers in 333 all mean something different based on where they are placed. *Children need to learn that 3 can mean 3, 30, or 300...and even higher.* They will need to remember what each position means (ones, tens, hundreds) and develop a sense of how many ones are in ten, how many tens are in a hundred, and so on.

One of the more challenging areas of place value is **regrouping**. When we regroup, we may gather ten ones to make a group of 10. Or we may take ten ones from the tens place, and bring them over to the ones place— sometimes this is referred to as "carrying" and "borrowing".

In order to understand what is happening when they cross off or carry numbers, kids need plenty of hands-on practice with objects that demonstrates what is happening when they regroup.

In first and second grades, kids will be building an important foundation for understanding place value. The more exploration they do now to make sense of this concept, the better they will understand how to work with larger numbers.

Place Value Skills Kids Need

Reading Numbers. Kids need to be able to read and name larger numbers like 58 or 297.

Comparing Numbers. They will need to look at two numbers and say which is greater or less. First graders will compare 2-digit numbers, while second graders should be able to compare 3-digit numbers.

Naming Place Value. When a second grader looks at a number like 267, she should be able to say which digit is in the hundreds place, the tens place, and the ones place.

Regrouping. You have 9 pennies. I give you 8 more. If you trade ten of your pennies for a dime, you are regrouping; you have traded in 10 ones for 1 ten. If you have 2 dimes and I need 12 cents, you will need to do some trading in pennies before you can give me exact change. Kids will need a lot of practice regrouping up and down with activities like these.

Regrouping in Addition or Subtraction. When adding 25+18, we regroup when we write the 3 and carry the 1. When subtracting 31-6 we regroup when we cross off the three, put a 2 above it, and turn the 1 into 11. Solving these written problems requires a combination of skills in place value, regrouping, adding, and subtracting.

While kids can learn to do these problems from rote memory, they will be much stronger in math if they understand what they are doing.

Place Value Counters

Many of the following games call for **place value counters.** These are objects that show kids the relationship between ones, tens, and sometimes hundreds and thousands.

The most common type of place value counters are called **base 10 blocks**. These are commercially-sold blocks that include small unit cubes, tens rods, hundreds flats, and a large thousands cube. Kids use these to make large numbers, visualize regrouping, and work with place value.

However, it isn't necessary to buy place value counters; with just a little preparation you can easily make your own. Here are a few examples:

24 bugs

13 clothespins

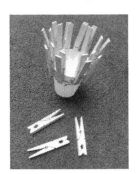

45 Q-tips

Represent hundreds by putting 10 ten-bundles (such as Q-tips bundled together with a rubber band) in a large plastic baggie. Place value counters are often used with place value mats, especially to solve addition or subtraction problems involving regrouping.

Place Value Games

Number Roll

Players: 2   **Skill:** place value, counting by 10s and 1s
Materials: place value counters, place value mats, 2-3 numeral dice, paper

1. Print a place value mat (from page 72) for each player, and point out the difference between the tens counters and the ones counters.

2. Take turns rolling two numeral dice (see "note", below). One of the dice will be used to show tens; the other die will show ones.

3. If you rolled a number 4 for tens and 2 for ones, put 4 tens counters in the 'tens' column and 2 ones counters in the 'ones' column. Say the name of the number and write it down.

4. Have both players leave their counters on their board to compare at the end of that round. Who got the highest number? The greater number wins the round.

5. NOTE: For this game, I recommend that instead of traditional dot dice you use *numeral dice*, like those shown here. When putting a 3 and a 4 next to each other with numeral dice, our eyes see 34, whereas with dot dice we are more likely to see the total number 7.

6. CHALLENGE: Use three numeral dice and add hundreds counters to make and compare larger numbers.

Add It On

Players: 2   **Skill:** place value, counting by 10s and 1s, regrouping
Materials: place value counters, place value mats, baggies, 2 numeral dice

1. Give each player a place value mat (page 72). Take turns rolling 2 numeral dice: one is 'ones' and the other is 'tens'. Make the number on your place value mat using the place value counters. For example, if you roll a 5 and a 3 you could make either 53 or 35 using counters.

2. (**Important**: Leave the counters on your mat while the other players take their turns. You will add to these counters on your next turn.)

3. When your turn comes around, roll again and make the new number with counters. Add these to the counters that were already on your mat.

4. Now, here is the most important part. See how many counters are in the 'ones' place. If you have more than 10 'ones', trade some of them in for one 'ten'. Move the new 'ten' counter to the 'tens' spot.

5. Have more than 10 tens? Trade ten of them in for a 'hundreds' counter and put this in the 'hundreds' spot.

6. Read your new number total. Play 5 turns, then count and compare final numbers. The highest number wins.

7. NOTE: For this game, I highly recommend that instead of traditional dot dice you use *numeral dice*, with the numbers written on them. This is because these dice can be lined up next to each other to resemble the numbers in their written form.

Slap Down

Players: 2+   **Skill:** place value, naming large numbers
Materials: playing cards with face cards removed

1. Remove the face cards (jack, queen, king) from the deck and tell kids that aces = 1. Place the deck face down in the middle of the table.

2. On their turn, have each player make a 3-digit number by taking three cards from the deck and laying them down to make a number: ex: 459.  Players will try to make the largest number possible with their cards.

3. Leave your cards out until the end of the round, so that everyone has a 3-digit number in front of them. Each person reads their number out loud. Players compare the numbers to see which is the highest.

4. The person with the greatest number wins that round. That player takes ALL the cards that were played by the other players, and puts these in a pile in front of her. These are her points.

5. When you have gone through the whole deck, each player counts their cards. The one with the most cards wins.

6. Adjust the level of the game by making 2-digit or 4-digit numbers.

7. NOTE: There are two learning challenges in this game: understanding how to make the largest possible number with three cards, and comparing three digit numbers. For more practice, give your child the coveted role of "judge" and let him be the one who compares numbers at the end of *every* round.

High Rollers

Players: 2-4   **Skill:** place value, naming numbers, regrouping (challenge)
Materials: 1 die, paper, pencils

1. Give each player a piece of paper and a pencil. Each person writes 3 lines on the paper, like this: ____ ____ ____ , where they will fill in a three-digit number.

2. The goal is to get the largest number for that round.

3. To play, take turns rolling the die one time. On each roll, fill in one of the lines on your paper with the number on the die. *Once a number is written down, it cannot be changed.*

4. Continue taking turns and rolling the die until everyone has filled in their 3-digit number. Have each person read their number out loud.

5. The highest number wins the round. The winner for that round circles his number. Play can continue as long as you want, with many potential winners.

6. NOTE: You can easily adjust the level of the game by making either two-digit or four-digit numbers.

7. CHALLENGE: Instead of circling numbers to mark "wins", you can also play for points. Play as above until each player has filled in three 3-digit numbers. Then have each player add their column of three numbers. This will likely involve some regrouping. Compare final scores; highest score wins.

Money: an overview

Money is an exciting topic for kids. They know that money is powerful, and that it gets them things. Whether they have their own money or not, you will find that they are very motivated to learn this particular skill!

That's good news for you, especially since counting money can be a bit complicated to master.

To play the money games in this book, you will need a good supply of coins. I suggest you go to the bank and ask for: $1 in pennies, $1 in nickels, $2-3 in dimes, and $2-3 in quarters. Real coins are way more interesting than play money! Keep the coins in a jar for money games and money practice.

(Kids may also want to "play" with the money on their own; encourage this! If they are stacking coins and making money trains, ask them which stack "costs" the most, or other questions that get them counting money.)

If you prefer to buy play money, just be sure you don't get a set with a bunch of paper money and not enough coins. Counting coins is the bigger challenge for first and second graders.

First graders can count pennies, nickels, dimes, or quarters by skip counting, but in the beginning don't mix different coin types.

By **second grade**, kids will learn to count coins using mixed skills, and will do written addition or subtraction problems with money.

Money Skills Kids Need

Identifying Coin Values. Children need to recognize both the front and back of a coin and say how much each is worth (ex: a penny=1 cent, nickel=5 cents, dime=10 cents, and so on).

Skip Counting. When counting anything other than pennies, kids need to know how to skip count by 5, 10, and 25 up to 100.

Counting On. Counting coins may require a child to skip count by 10s (dimes) up to a point, then count on remaining pennies. A child with 3 dimes and 2 pennies would count: 10, 20, 30... 31, 32.

Putting Coins in Order. Before adding mixed coins, it is important to separate them by value and put the coins in order from high to low. Quarters are added first, then dimes, nickels and pennies.

Mixed Counting Skills. A handful of coins might include 2 quarters, a dime, 3 nickels and a penny. To count these, children must sort them, put them in order high to low, and count. Start with the quarters: 25, 50. Add the dime and count on: 60. Nickels: 65, 70, 75. And finally the penny: 76.

Adding, Subtracting, and Regrouping. When adding or subtracting anything above a dollar, kids will need place value and regrouping skills. They will also be introduced to decimals, and how to bring the decimal down when doing written addition or subtraction problems.

Money Games

Dollar Race

Players: 2   **Skill:** counting money, adding money, regrouping with coins
Materials: 2 dice, real or play money (pennies, dimes, dollars)

1. First, create a "bank" with pennies, dimes, and a dollar.

2. Take turns rolling 2 dice and counting up the total. The total number indicates the amount of money you can take for that roll. If you roll a total of 9, have a child take 9 pennies from the bank and put them in front of you.

3. I recommend having a child be the "banker" and count out money for all the players. Kids will get more practice this way.

4. Whenever you get more than 10 pennies, trade them in for a dime. The first to get to $1.00 wins.

5. NOTE: Playing just with pennies and dimes reinforces the regrouping skills they are learning for place value.

6. VARIATION: You could also stock the bank with pennies, nickels, dimes and quarters. To play this way, the rule would be that you must make your number using the *fewest possible number of coins*. Kids can occasionally trade in smaller coins for higher-valued coins to make counting easier, but playing this way does make the place value relationship of regrouping ones and tens less clear.

Coin Count Combos

Players: 2+   **Skill:** counting money, using different combinations of coins
Materials: 2 dice, real or play money (coins), paper and pencil

1. On your turn, roll the dice and count the total. Then count out that number of cents using coins. For example, let's say that Jim rolls a 6 and a 5, for a total of 11 cents.

2. Jim needs to use some combination of coins to make that total. He chooses to use a dime and a penny. He puts his 11 cents in front of him.

3. The next player tries to make 11 cents using a *new* combination of coins. Let's say he chooses two nickels and a penny.

4. Play continues as long as the next person can show 11 cents a new way. Eventually players will run out of new ways to make 11 cents. When this happens, the last person who was able to show 11 cents with a new combination of coins scores an *extra* 10 cents.

5. The person who was not able to make 11 cents in a new way rolls the dice again and gets a new total. She uses coins to make the new number, and play continues. The game ends when someone gets to 50 cents.

6. NOTE: This is a great game for helping kids get comfortable with various ways of counting money, as well as flexibility in adding and subtracting. Eleven can be a dime and a penny, two nickels and a penny, six pennies and a nickel, or simply eleven pennies—all addition problems that add up to the same number.

Buried Treasure

Players: 2+   **Skill:** counting coins
Materials: a bag of rice, coins, medium container, scoop, bowls, paper

1. Fill a container with uncooked rice. Dump in a quantity of mixed coins, and mix up the coins and rice together. Give each player an empty bowl. Put a measuring scoop in with the rice/coins mixture. A 1/4 cup scoop is a good size to start.

2. The first player takes a scoop out of the big container and puts it in his bowl. He finds the coins in his "buried treasure", counts the amount of money he found, then writes the total as his score for that round. The other players do the same.

3. Play 5 rounds, then have each person add up their totals. See which player got the highest amount.

4. COOPERATIVE VERSION: Instead of seeing who gets the highest score, put all your "treasure" in a pile and count how much everyone got. In addition to making everyone be a winner, it also allows kids to count quite a bit higher when adding up all the coins.

5. NOTE: You can control the degree of challenge by how big the scoops are, or by your choice of which coins to mix in. If kids are learning to count by 5, put in only nickels. Or put in dimes and pennies only. You can also vary the size of the scoop to get more or less money to count.

Money in the Bank

Players: 2   **Skill:** counting, adding and subtracting coins, regrouping
Materials: deck of cards, coins, paper and pencil (optional)

1. Take the face cards (jacks, queens and kings) out of the deck of cards.

2. Divide the deck in two and give half to each player, face down. Give each player 30 cents to start with. Put additional coins to one side. This is the "bank".

3. Players take turns flipping over a card. **If the card is black, give yourself that much money from the bank.** For example, if I turn over a black 10, I can take a dime from the bank.

4. **If the card is red, you have to pay the bank** that much money. If you turn up a red 4, you pay the bank 4 cents. (You can teach kids the expression "in the red", which means you owe money.) Keep track of points by adding or subtracting them on each round.

5. There are two ways to win. If a player reaches 60 points, that person wins the game. Or, if one person runs out of money, the other person wins the game.

6. CHALLENGE: Most kids will simply re-count all their money after each round. For more of a challenge, have kids write their current total on their paper, then add or subtract the number on their newest card to find their new total. Adding and subtracting money on paper uses different skills than those used when adding, subtracting and counting the coins themselves.

Fractions: an overview

Fractions are a way to talk about **pieces or parts of things**. When we cut something into pieces, we divide it up, either in half (1/2) or in other ways (such as fourths). Even though fractions and division look different on paper, the concepts are very much the same.

The bottom number of a fraction (denominator) tells you how many pieces a thing has been divided into. The top number (numerator) says how many of those pieces we are talking about.

There are actually two kinds of fractions. We can divide up one thing by cutting it, such as cutting a pizza into 8 pieces. Our fraction tells us the **parts of one whole**, such as eating 2/8 of the pizza.

We can also divide up things, like cookies. If we bake 12 cookies and then divide them up, we each get **a part of the total** number of cookies. If you eat 3 cookies, you will have eaten 3/12 of them.

Notice and **talk with kids about fractions** as often as you can. Cut a sandwich into fourths and point out that fourths use 4 pieces of the same size. When your child pours half a cup of milk into cookie batter, show that it takes two of these to make one cup. When you divide a deck of cards in two, point out that each person has half of the cards.

Kids will need lots of opportunities to use fractions and talk about them before the concept will begin to make sense.

Fraction Skills Kids Need

Concept of Equal Parts. Children may know that 1/4 is one of four pieces, without understanding that each part has to be exactly the same size. If something isn't shared or divided equally, it is not a fraction.

Recognizing Fractions. Children will learn to look at a drawing of a fraction and say what fraction it represents. Start with 1/2, 1/3, and 1/4, and branch out into other types of fractions later on.

Reading Fractions. Before kids can read and name fractions, they will need to know their ordinal numbers: words like "third, fourth, fifth" and so on. They will learn that 1/2 is not read as "one-second", but one-half. Some kids may be able to read fractions without understanding their meaning.

Comparing Fractions. When looking at two drawings or models of fractions, kids should be able to say which one is greater, or whether they are equal (such as 2/4 and 1/2). In second grade they will compare written fractions with the same numerator (1/4 and 1/5), or the same denominator (1/3 and 2/3).

Ordering Fractions. Second graders, when given a list of fractions with the same numerator such as 3/6, 3/4, and 3/5, will be asked to put them in order from least to greatest. They may also be asked to order fractions with the same denominator: 3/4, 1/4, 2/4. Showing the fractions using fraction strips or another representation will be a big help as kids learn this skill.

Fractions Games

The Half Game

Players: 2-4   **Skill:** fractions, understanding half, odd and even numbers

Materials: dried beans or counters, deep bowl, paper, pencil, large spoon

1. Put a bunch of dried beans or other counters in a bag or deep bowl. On your turn, use a large spoon to scoop out as many beans as you can.

2. Count the beans you scooped out, and pair them up to see if the total is odd or even. Does every bean have a partner? If so, divide your beans in half and count them. The half number is your score—write down your score for that round.

3. What if you drew an odd number of beans? You can't divide them in half (without cutting a bean), so you don't get a score that round, but leave your beans on the table. This is where things get interesting!

4. The next player scoops out another spoonful of beans and *adds them to yours on the table*. The beans get put in pairs. Are they odd or even?

5. If the number is even, she gets half that big number as her score. BUT-- if the number is odd (that is, if the beans don't match up evenly in pairs), then the next player scoops out even more beans and adds them to the pile! Play until someone reaches 100 points.

Egg Carton Fractions

Players: 2   **Skill:** comparing fractions, writing fractions

Materials: 2 empty egg cartons, 12 dried beans or counters, paper, pencil

1. Before starting the game, explore egg carton fractions with your child. There are 12 cups in the carton, so all your fractions will have 12 on the bottom. Fill up just a few cups to make fractions, such as 3/12. Say and write the fractions you make together.

2. When your child has a grasp of how egg carton fractions work, put 12 counters in the egg carton, one in each egg cup. Your fraction is 12/12 because there is a counter in every cup. Close the lid, and shake it up!

3. Open up the egg carton and see how many of the 12 cups the counters landed in. If counters land in 5 cups, write 5/12.

4. The next person takes a turn shaking his carton and writes the fraction.

5. Put the two cartons side by side and compare the fractions. Who got the larger fraction for that round? That person gets ten points.

6. Continue making and comparing fractions until someone gets 50 points.

7. NOTE: While you could pass one carton back and forth, I prefer using 2 egg cartons with young kids. This way, kids see both fractions at once to compare them, as well as comparing the written numbers. The extra visual is helpful when dealing with this somewhat tricky concept.

Fraction Cover-Up

Players: 2   **Skill:** fractions concepts, comparing fractions, addition

Materials: two sets of fraction strips with two "wholes" each, one die

1. Give each player his or her own set of fraction strips, each with two "whole" pieces in front of them. The fraction pieces are put to the side.

2. The object of the game is to be the first person to **fill two wholes** exactly with fraction pieces.

3. Roll the die to collect fraction pieces. A 2 is one-half, 3 is one-third, 4 is one-fourth, and 6 is one-sixth. If you roll a 1 or a 5, roll again. If you cannot use the fraction you rolled, skip that turn.

4. Each time you collect a fraction piece, add it to one of your "wholes". (Each whole must be finished exactly--players can't go over.)

5. After playing for a while, kids will notice that certain types of fractions don't fit together evenly to make a whole. Players are allowed to move their fraction pieces freely between the two wholes to make the pieces add up evenly to one.

6. While playing, encourage kids to compare their fractions and talk about what they notice. "Look, my 1/2 is the same as two of my 1/4 pieces."

7. NOTE: Let kids discover on their own that certain fraction pieces don't fit together, and to try and fix the problem themselves. If they are not getting it on their own, suggest they try trading pieces between wholes to see if they fit better.

Uncover It

Players: 2   **Skill:** comparing fractions, subtraction, regrouping

Materials: two sets of fraction strips with 2 wholes, one die

1. This game is the exact opposite of Fraction Cover-Up. It is challenging because it involves subtraction and regrouping of fractions.

2. To set up the game, each player lays out both "whole" pieces. Cover one with two halves, and the other with three thirds.

3. Players take turns rolling the die to remove fractions. A rolled 2 is one-half, 3 is one-third, 4 is one-fourth, and 6 is one-sixth. If you get 1 or a 5, roll again.

4. On your turn, roll the die. If you get a 3, take 1/3 off of one of your wholes, if you can.

5. However, what if you roll a 4 and you just have two 1/2's? You could trade a half for two fourths. Then you could take away 1/4.

6. Continue removing fractions/regrouping till someone gets to 0 exactly.

7. NOTE: It can be hard for kids to know what to trade when they need to regroup. You may want to write down on a piece of paper what they can trade: one 1/3 for two 1/6s; one 1/2 for two 1/4s. When kids roll a number that they don't have on their sheet, they can refer to the paper to see what they might trade.

Multiplication: an overview

First and second grade math will lay the ground work for learning multiplication. It is important that kids have a solid understanding of this concept, because they will spend the next several years building on it.

Multiplication can be thought of as repeated addition. 6 x 3 is the same as 6+6+6. It is helpful to let kids use objects to show three groups of six before adding them together. Point out that the groups are all the same size, which means you can skip count: 6, 12, 18. Six times three is 18.

Help kids get familiar with the **language of multiplication** even before they are ready to multiply on their own. Talk about equal groups, skip counting, "times" and multiplication. When kids begin to read actual multiplication problems, it is a good practice to have them read the "x" as "groups of". 6 x 3 is six groups of 3, and 3 x 6 is three groups of 6.

A term that will come up often in early multiplication is **arrays**. Arrays are sets of objects in equal rows, a visual representation of multiplication. This array could show 3 x 4 or 4 x 3.

You might be tempted to jump into helping kids memorize times tables. Before you do, make sure your child has a firm grasp of addition and subtraction facts first. Play hands-on games that let kids see what multiplication is all about. Practice skip counting. If any of these are weak, don't move on to the times tables yet. Make sure their foundation is strong; if it is, later multiplication skills will come all the more quickly.

Multiplication Skills Kids Need

Concept of Equal Parts. To multiply, all the groups must be exactly the same quantity. This can be a hard concept for kids to grasp. Give lots of practice showing multiplication with objects to drive home this fact.

Skip Counting. Counting by 2's, 3's, 4's, and other numbers up to 10 is one of the most important foundational skills for learning to multiply. In the beginning, kids will skip count by repeated addition. Later, they should be able to quickly skip count any number (between 2 and 10) ten times.

Language of Multiplication. Kids will need to understand and use vocabulary such as "times", "multiply", "groups of", "product" and "arrays". The best way to get kids comfortable with new vocabulary is to use it often. Use these terms as a natural part of playing the multiplication games, and ask kids what their "product" was, or to draw an array.

Writing Multiplication Problems. Kids will learn to look at a drawing, such as 2 groups of 4 frogs, and write a multiplication sentence about it: 2 x 4. They will also solve written problems using drawings or objects.

Multiplication Facts. Kids will learn multiplication facts, in the beginning, by skip counting while counting on their fingers. This is slower than memorization, but is entirely appropriate for their age. Make sure kids understand the relationship of multiplication to skip counting before beginning to memorize. Start with 2s, 5s, and 10s, and move on from there.

Multiplication Games

Pigs in a Pen

Players: 2+   **Skill:** multiplication, adding, counting

Materials: at least 6 rubber bands, dried beans, 2 dice, paper and pencil

1. Set aside at least six medium or large rubber bands and a bowl full of dried beans. Roll one of the dice, and look at the number. Put that many rubber bands in front of you. These are "pig pens".

2. Roll the other die and read the number. Put that many beans (pigs) inside each rubber band (pen).

3. Read the problem: "Four pens with three pigs. 4 times 3."

4. Get the total number of pigs in whichever way makes the most sense for your child's age and skill level: counting, skip counting, or multiplying.

5. Say the problem with the answer: "4 times 3 is 12". Write down the total (12) as your score for that round.

6. NOTE: Even though this is a multiplication game, it can be played by young learners as well, who will form the problems and count to get the answers. Older kids will skip-count to find the total, while advanced learners may multiply in their heads and then check their answer.

7. As they get better at these skills, challenge them to find the total without counting every bean.

Crowded Rectangles

Players: 2   **Skill:** multiplication, drawing arrays

Materials: a piece of graph paper, pencil, 2 dice

1. Put a sheet of graph paper (the kind with squares) on the table in front of you. The kind with larger squares is easier for young children and the game goes faster, but any kind will do.

2. Roll both dice, then use both of the numbers in a multiplication problem. Ex: "two times three".

2×3

3. On the graph paper, make a box that is 2 squares tall and 3 squares across. Count the squares inside. The amount of squares inside the box is the answer to the problem.

4. Inside the box, write the multiplication problem 2 x 3 = 6.

5. The next player rolls, says a different problem, and draws another box anywhere on the graph paper.

6. Players take turns rolling and drawing boxes. As they play, the paper will get more and more crowded with squares. There will come a time when someone will roll a number that will not fit in a square on the paper. When this happens, the game ends.

7. The last person to make a box on the paper wins.

8. FINISH QUICKER: If your graph paper has a lot of small squares and it looks like you will be playing for a VERY long time, just fold part of the paper over to make your "playing field" smaller.

Buzz

Players: 2+   **Skill:** multiplication, counting, skip counting

Materials: none

1. This is a spoken game that can be played anywhere, since it uses no materials. It does require some concentration, though.

2. Choose a number your child feels comfortable multiplying by, such as 5. Before playing the game, review skip counting by 5's.

3. To play the game, the first person says "one". The second person says "two". The next person says "three". Players continue taking turns saying a number, counting up in sequence.

4. Here's the catch: when you get to a number that is a multiple of 5, that person says "buzz" instead of saying the number.

5. The next person continues with the next number.

6. So as an example, if you are doing "fives", players would take turns saying the numbers, and it would go like this: "One. Two. Three. Four. Buzz. Six. Seven. Eight. Nine. Buzz." (And so on.)

7. Play as a team challenge to see how high your group can get.

8. NOTE: This is an easy game to get the concept of, but it can be tricky to play. I suggest starting with 2's to let kids get a feel for the game. This will quickly become easy, and you can move on to 5's or 10's. As your child becomes more proficient in skip counting, add 3's or 4's.

Skippy

Players: 2+   **Skill:** multiplication, skip counting, adding and regrouping

Materials: 2 dice, paper, pencil, beans or other counters (optional)

1. NOTE: Before playing this game, make sure your child is comfortable with the basic concept of multiplication. The game "Skippy" uses multiplication facts up to 6's, but kids who don't know the facts by heart can skip count or use counters to figure out the answer.

2. Roll the two dice and say the multiplication problem: 4 times 2.

3. Figure out the multiplication problem any way you know how: by skip counting, using counters, or remembering multiplication facts.

4. Write down the total as your score.

5. After 5 rounds, have everyone add their scores. There is likely to be some regrouping needed as kids add their totals.

6. The highest score wins.

7. NOTE: One of the nice things about this game is that multiplication problems don't go higher than 6 x 6. This gives kids a chance to work on memorizing the lower multiplication tables, and is also easier to handle if kids are using counters to figure out their answers.

Appendix

- Glossary

- Printables and Resources

- Hundreds Chart

- Place Value Mat

- Number Line 1-100

- Fraction Strips

- Number Cards

- Skip Counting

- Game Finder

- Alphabetical Index

- About the Author

Glossary

array: A group of objects or images that are arranged in equal rows and columns, to make a rectangle.

base 10 blocks: These blocks help kids see the relationship between ones, tens, hundreds and thousands. Ones are small squares, tens are rods, hundreds are flats, and thousands are cubes. The blocks are often used with place value mats.

counting back: Starting at a number other than one, and counting backwards from there. For example, subtracting three from 35, you'd count back: 34, 33, 32.

counting on: Starting at a number other than one, and counting upwards from there. For example, adding three to 35, you'd count on: 36, 37, 38.

counters: Any small objects that can be used to physically show counting, adding, or other basic calculations. Counters can be almost anything (beans, buttons, plastic bears) but should be easy for small hands to handle.

denominator: The bottom number of a fraction, ex: in 3/4 the denominator is 4. The denominator tells us how many equal pieces an object or group has been divided into.

die: Two number cubes are called dice; one is called a die.

difference: We find the difference between two numbers by subtracting the smaller number from the larger one. The answer to a subtraction problem such as 12-6 is called the difference.

even number: Even numbers can be paired up exactly. When counting eight beans, kids who give each bean a "friend" will find that all 8 beans have a friend, so 8 is even. Even numbers all end in 2, 4, 6, 8 or 0.

fact family: A set of numbers with related addition and subtraction problems. For example, 2+3=5 comes from the fact family 2, 3, 5. These same numbers can also make the problems 3+2=5, 5-2=3, and 5-3=2.

fraction: Fractions can be part of a group or a piece of a whole. When a fraction is part of a group, we write the total number in the group on the bottom, and the amount we are talking about on top. So if there are 8 blocks and we share 4 of them, each person has 4/8 of the blocks.

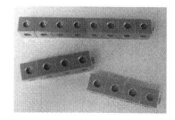

When we talk about a fraction as a piece of a whole, we first divide the whole into a certain number of pieces, and write that number on the bottom. If a pizza is cut into 4 pieces, and you eat 1 of them, you have eaten 1/4 of the pizza.

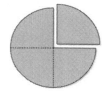

hundreds chart: A chart that has the numbers from 1 to 100 written in order. The first row is 1-10, the second row 11-20, and so on. This tool helps kids see relationships between numbers when counting, skip counting, subtracting, etc.

math facts: Simple math problems that kids must know automatically in order to solve harder problems, such as 3+2 and 8-5. Kids will need to memorize addition and subtraction facts to 20 and, later, multiplication facts to 100.

numerator: The top number of a fraction that tells the part we are talking about: **2**/3. The numerator (2) tells us we're talking about 2 of the 3 parts.

odd number: Numbers that cannot be exactly paired up. When kids are given 7 beans and asked to put them in pairs, there is one extra that "does not have a friend", so the number is odd. Odd numbers end in 1, 3, 5, 7 or 9.

place value: All numbers are made using only ten digits: 0-9. Most numbers are combinations of these digits. How much each digit is worth changes depending on if it is in the 1's place, the 10's place, the 100's place, and so on.

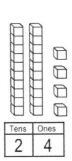

A numeral's position in a number is called its place value. For example, in the number 555, we only use one digit, a five, but in one position we read 500, in the next position we read 50, and in the final position we read 5.

place value counters: Any objects that can represent ones, tens, and hundreds can be used as place value counters. Base 10 blocks are great, but you can easily make your own. (These Q-tip counters show the number 45.) You can also use dried beans, leaving 1's loose, putting 10's in small cups, and putting 100's in clear plastic baggies. For more ideas, see page 40.

place value mat (or chart): A mat that visually divides the ones, tens, and sometimes hundreds places, to help teach place value. Kids can use place value counters to represent numbers on the mat.

Tens	Ones

For example, to make the number 35 on this mat, kids would put 3 tens counters on the "tens" side, and 5 ones counters on the "ones" side.

regrouping: When solving a problem like 72-19, we can't subtract 2-9, so we have to regroup. We borrow ten from the 70 so we can subtract 12-9. Whenever we borrow numbers in a subtraction problem, or carry numbers in addition, we are regrouping.

$$
\begin{array}{r}
{\scriptstyle 4}{\scriptstyle 1} \\
\cancel{5}\ 1 \\
-\ \ 8 \\
\hline
4\ 3
\end{array}
$$

rounding: Numbers like 30, 80, or 200 are easier to picture in our minds than 76 or 192. When we scoot exact numbers into their nearest tens or hundreds position, we have rounded these numbers.

skip counting: Counting by 2s (2, 4, 6, 8), by 5s (5, 10, 15, 20), by 3s (3, 6, 9, 12), or any other number is called skip counting because you skip over certain numbers. Skip counting is faster than regular counting, and is an important step in learning to multiply.

sum: When we solve an addition problem, the answer is called the sum.

Printables and Resources

There are a few math tools that make a really big difference in helping first and second graders understand math concepts. Most of those used in this book are included here in the Appendix or in the body of this book, and you can access the complete set of PDF downloads through the *Miss Brain's Cool Math Games* website at www.coolmathgamesforkids1-2.com:

- Hundreds Chart
- Number Line 1-100
- Place Value Mat
- Skip Counting Reference
- Fraction Strips
- Make Your Own Fraction Strips
- Two-Digit Number Cards
- Place Value Counters

Along with these printables, you will find a list of the materials used in this book at the *Miss Brain's Cool Math Games* website. Whether you prefer to print materials, make your own, or buy a sturdy set of reusable math tools, the "Resources" section will steer you toward what you need.

http://www.coolmathgamesforkids1-2.com

Hundreds Chart

1	2	3	4	5	6	7	8	9	10
11	12	13	14	15	16	17	18	19	20
21	22	23	24	25	26	27	28	29	30
31	32	33	34	35	36	37	38	39	40
41	42	43	44	45	46	47	48	49	50
51	52	53	54	55	56	57	58	59	60
61	62	63	64	65	66	67	68	69	70
71	72	73	74	75	76	77	78	79	80
81	82	83	84	85	86	87	88	89	90
91	92	93	94	95	96	97	98	99	100

Ones	Tens

Number Line 1-100

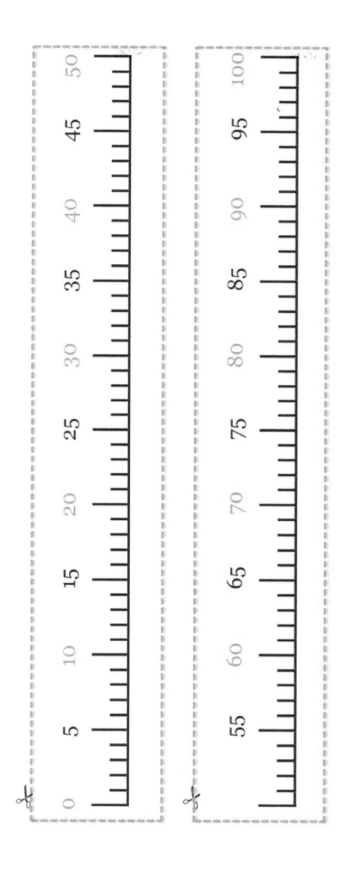

Directions: Cut out both number lines. Overlap and tape them together at #50 so you have one long number line that goes from 1-100.

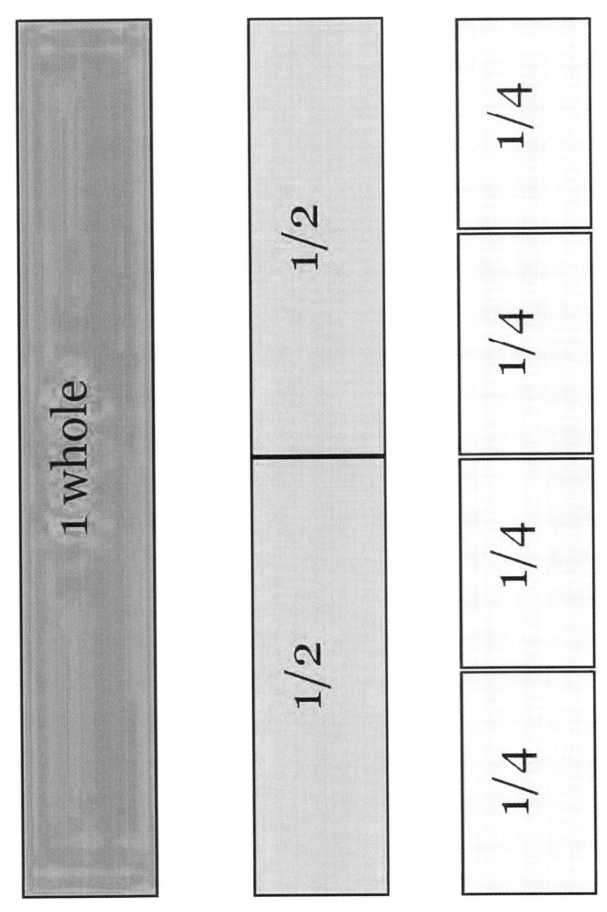

1 whole

1/3	1/3	1/3

1/6	1/6	1/6	1/6	1/6	1/6

Number Cards

10	11	12	13	14
15	16	17	18	19
20	22	24	26	28
31	33	35	37	39
40	42	44	46	48
51	53	55	57	59
60	62	64	66	68
71	73	75	77	79
80	82	84	86	88
91	93	95	97	99

Skip Counting

2's: 2, 4, 6, 8, 10, 12, 14, 16, 18, 20

3's: 3, 6, 9, 12, 15, 18, 21, 24, 27, 30

4's: 4, 8, 12, 16, 20, 24, 28, 32, 36, 40

5's: 5, 10, 15, 20, 25, 30, 35, 40, 45, 50

6's: 6, 12, 18, 24, 30, 36, 42, 48, 54, 60

7's: 7, 14, 21, 28, 35, 42, 49, 56, 63, 70

8's: 8, 16, 24, 32, 40, 48, 56, 64, 72, 80

9's: 9, 18, 27, 36, 45, 54, 63, 72, 81, 90

10's: 10, 20, 30, 40, 50, 60, 70, 80, 90

11's: 11, 22, 33, 44, 55, 66, 77, 88, 99

Game Finder

Even though the games in this book are organized by math area, there is a lot of overlap, since few skills are totally isolated. Kids practice counting, for example, not just in the "counting games", but in lots of other games as well. This game finder lets you know all your game options in each math area.

Number Sense

Whose Is Greater (16)
Twins (17)
Dozens Dice (18)
Guess Odd, Guess Even (19)
Odd and Even Beans (20)
The Odd-Even Game (21)
Giganto Score (21)
Roundit (22)
Addition War (31)
Subtraction War (35)

Number Roll (41)
Add It On (42)
High Rollers (44)
Slap Down (43)
Half Game (53)
Egg Carton Fractions (54)
Fraction Cover Up (55)
Uncover It (56)
(and probably a few more)

Counting

Dozens Dice (18)
Guess Odd, Guess Even (19)
Pig (25)
Tally Marks (26)
Make 10 (27)
Take It to Ten (27)
Bull's Eye (30)
Addition War (31)
Shut the Box (32)
Run to 100 (32)

Number Roll (41)
Add It On (42)
Dollar Race (47)
Coin Count Combos (48)
Buried Treasure (49)
Money in the Bank (50)
Pigs in a Pen (59)
Crowded Rectangles (60)
Buzz (61)
Skippy (62)

Addition

Dozens Dice (18)
Pig (25)
Make 10 (27)
Take It To Ten (27)
Bull's Eye (30)
Addition War (31)
Shut the Box (32)

Run to 100 (32)
Start With Ten (36)
Dollar Race (47)
Fraction Cover-Up (55)
Pigs in a Pen (59)
Skippy (62)

Subtraction

Place Value

Money

Fractions

Multiplication

Alphabetical Index of Games

About the Author

 Kelli Pearson (aka Miss Brain) has been making learning fun for kids for over 20 years. Her kids have explored the world of learning through math games, kids' clubs, children's musicals, science camps, creative writing workshops, and lots more.

Kelli is passionate about helping kids "get it", especially when it involves getting their bodies moving and their brain cells jumping. Her hands-on teaching style is especially powerful for kids with learning differences or attention issues who need to see or touch in order to understand.

You can find lots more hands-on learning activities and ideas at her website: **www.smartfirstgraders.com**. To book Kelli to do a Math Games Workshop or teacher training, or to learn about her kids' classes in the San Francisco bay area, visit **www.growingsmartkids.com**.

If you liked this book, please help spread the word. Write a review on Amazon, tell your friends on Facebook, or tweet your peeps!

Kelli loves to connect with her readers. If you have a success story or a suggestion to share, feel free to email kelli@growingsmartkids.com.

Made in the USA
Lexington, KY
06 May 2013